BACH
FOR BEGINNERS

BOOKS 1 AND 2

Compiled by Charles Vincent

ISBN 978-1-61780-496-0

by Elias   4)

T0079540

BOOSEY & HAWKES

AN IMAGEM COMPANY

DISTRIBUTED BY

HAL•LEONARD®
CORPORATION
7777 W. BLUEMOUND RD. P.O. BOX 13819 MILWAUKEE, WI 53213

www.boosey.com
www.halleonard.com

Preface to Book 1

For many years the study and practice of the works composed by J.S. Bach have been considered indispensable to all pianists and organists, but only in a few instances have attempts been made to introduce, to absolute beginners, the educational advantages to be derived from a study of the works of this great musician and teacher.

Bach took great delight in the musical education of his own family. When his eldest son W. Friedemann was 9 years old the father gave him lessons and wrote for him *The Little Clavier Book*, later we read of him giving lessons to his second wife Anna Magdalena, who became her husband's diligent pupil in clavier playing. Together they kept a musical note book in which were written her favorite pieces, also the various studies and airs the husband composed for her to practice.

A careful perusal of this "Note Book" has suggested the compilation of a series of graded material for beginners, the first book to be selected entirely from this very interesting "Note Book."

Bach had seven children by his first wife and thirteen by his second, so Anna Magdalena must have had much to occupy her time besides studying the lessons her husband composed for her, yet it is recorded that she was musically of the greatest possible help to him. She had a beautiful voice and many of his finest songs were written for her. She was 21 years of age when they were married on December 3, 1721.

Charles Vincent

Preface to Book 2

No finer material exists, on which to train a musician, than that to be found in the compositions of J.S. Bach — independence of the hands and fingers, correct part playing, careful expression, and freedom of execution being absolutely necessary in the performance of his works.

In this series entitled *Bach for Beginners* the editor has made an effort to carefully grade the several numbers so that progress may be easy and assured.

Book 1 contains material taken from *Anna Magdalena's Note Book*, Bach's second wife.

Book 2 consists chiefly of numbers taken from *The Little Clavier Book*, which Bach began in 1720 for his little son W. Friedemann Bach, aged 9, when instructing him in the art of clavier playing, as well as some pieces of suitable difficulty selected from his other works written for educational purposes.

Compositions for the clavichord and harpsichord abound in adornments, trills and mordents, but however effective some of these were upon the clavier they are not all capable of equally effective interpretation on the pianoforte.

In this book up to and including No. 27, whenever such ornaments occur they are written out in full in the music. Nos. 28 and 29 have the signs exactly as Bach wrote them. Before No. 28 however is an explanation of these signs with which it is most necessary every student of Bach's works must become familiar.

At the beginning of *The Little Clavier Book* Bach wrote out the ornaments with an explanation for his son, and immediately followed with a little study he named "Applicatio," intended as an exercise and an illustration of these ornaments, this study appears as No. 28 in this collection.

It is interesting to note that Bach was a pioneer of modern fingering, previous to his time the thumb was almost excluded from use, while the little finger was but seldom employed — Nos. 28 and 29 contain the fingering exactly as Bach wrote it for his son, and No. 29 would not be fingered differently even in the present day.

Charles Vincent

CONTENTS
Book 1

Book 2

BACH FOR BEGINNERS
Book 1: *Anna Magdalena's Note Book*

Lied

Selected, Phrased and Fingered by
CHARLES VINCENT

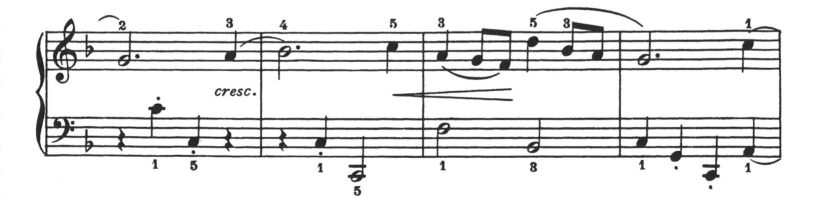

Lied
The Smoker's reflections

This song, evidently a favorite of Bach's, also appears a second time
in the "Note Book" transposed a fourth higher to suit his wife's voice.
The following is a translation of the words of the first verse:

Whenever in an hour of leisure
With Knaster good my pipe I fill,
And sit and smoke for rest or pleasure,
Sad pictures rise without my will.
Watching the clouds of smoke float by
I think how like this pipe am I.

Chorale

Many beautiful chorales were composed by Bach, and he made use of
choral themes to a great extent in his compositions, many of his most
ingenious and enjoyable works being founded on melodies of this type.
He also employed chorales as a means of education.

Minuet

No. 4

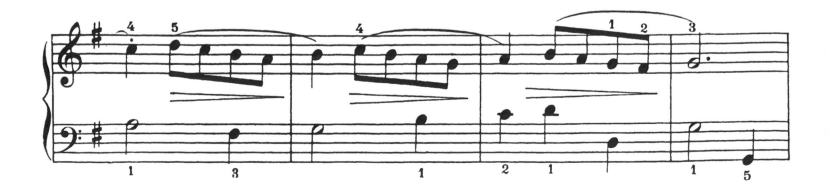

Minuet in G minor

No. 5

Minuet in G Major

MONS BÖHM

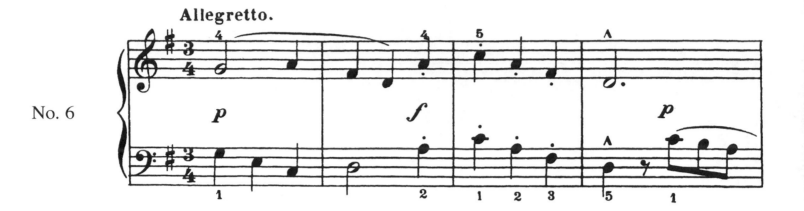

No. 6

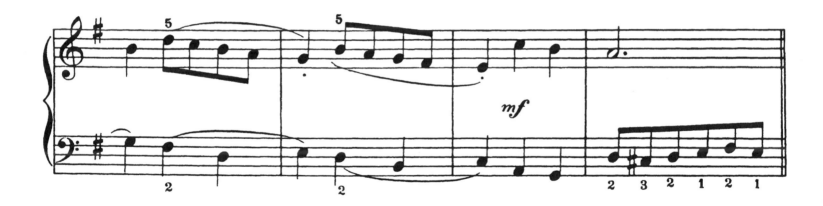

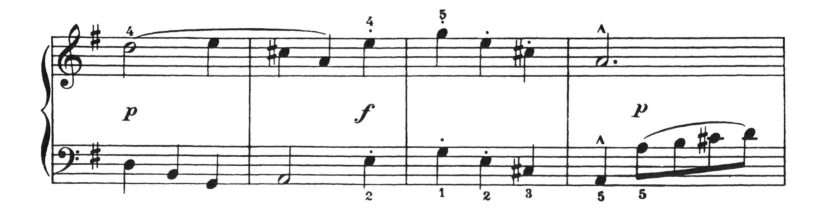

This minuet is by a Mons Böhm, but its insertion in the
"Note Book" proves it to have been a favorite with the
Bachs, which is sufficient reason for its inclusion here.

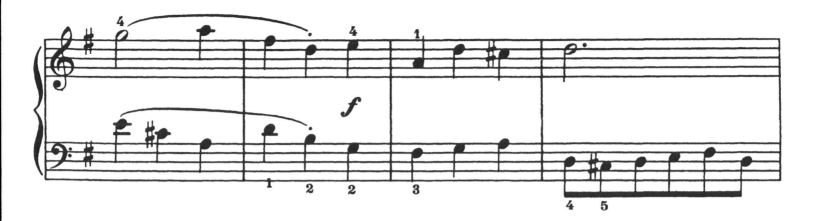
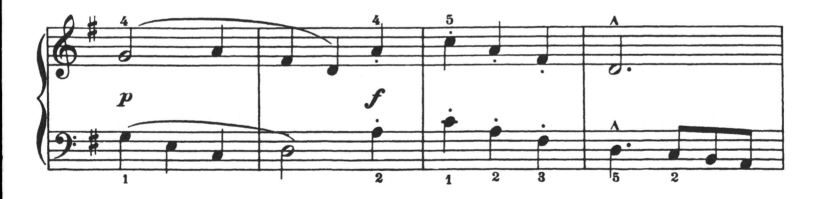

Minuet in G Major

No. 7

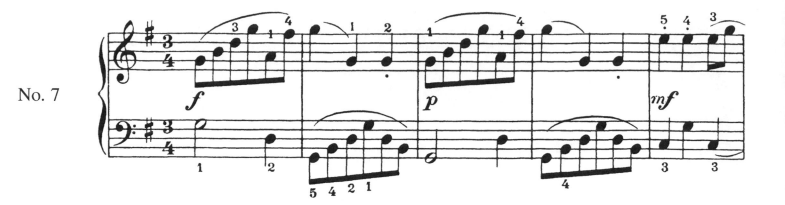

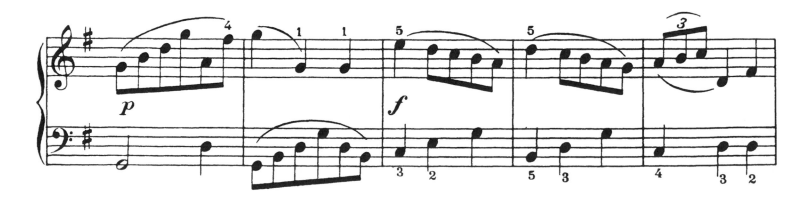

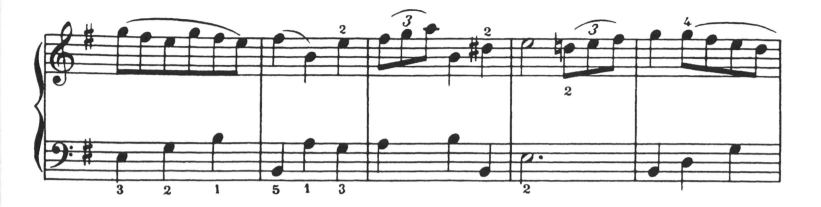

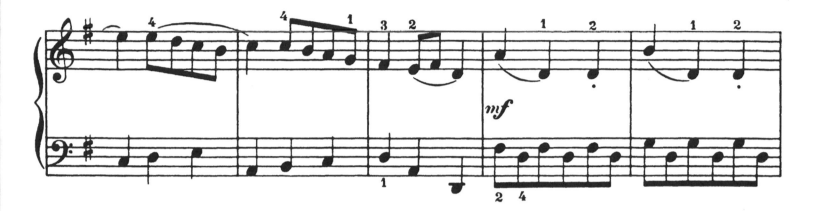

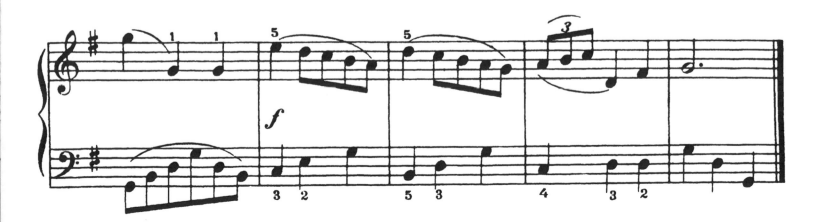

Chorale

Eternity, O mighty word

No. 8

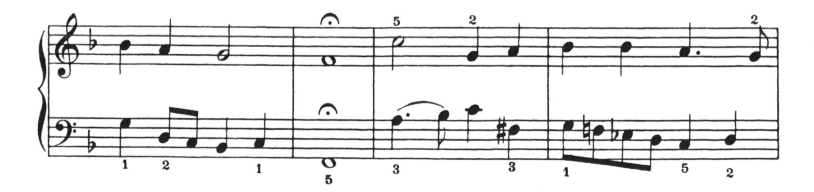

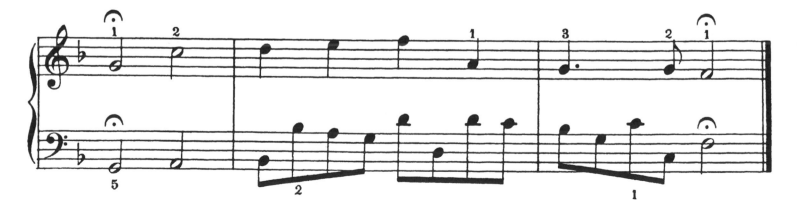

See note to No. 3 on page 7.

Polonaise

Moderato.

No. 9

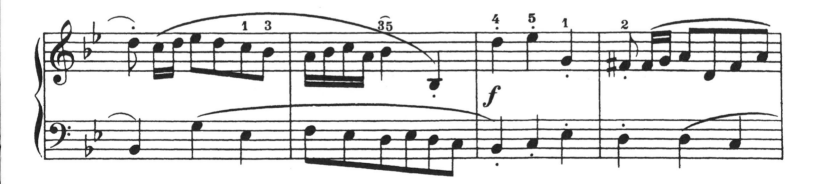

March in D Major

No. 10

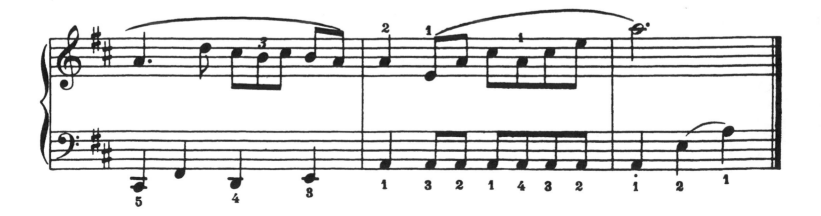

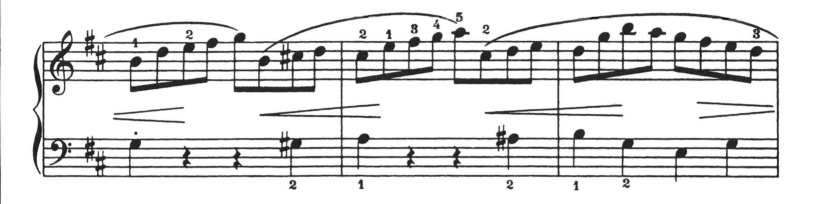

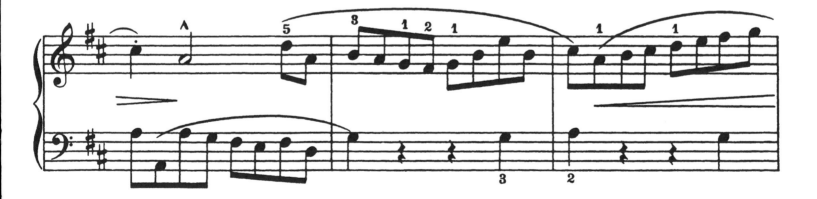

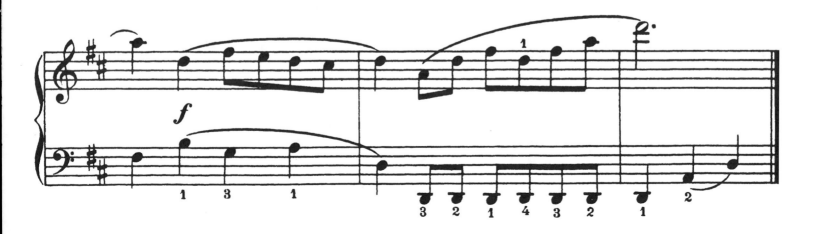

Musette

No. 11

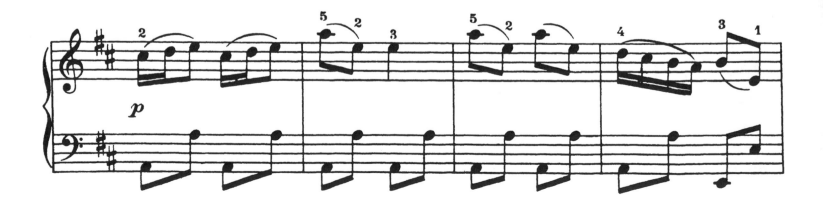

Echo

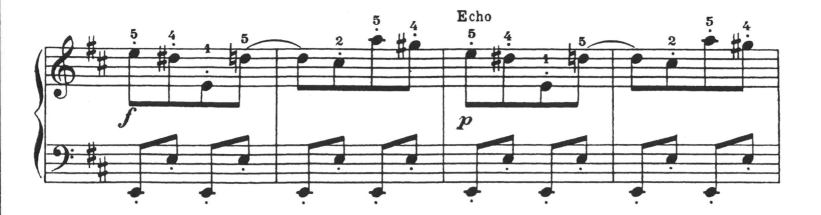

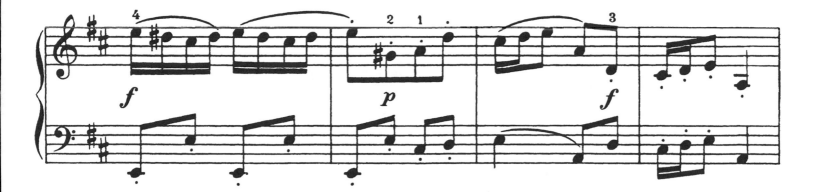

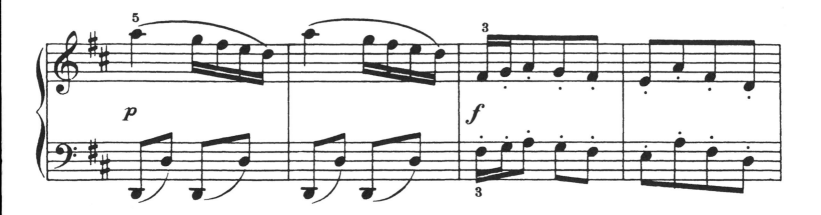

Minuet

No. 12

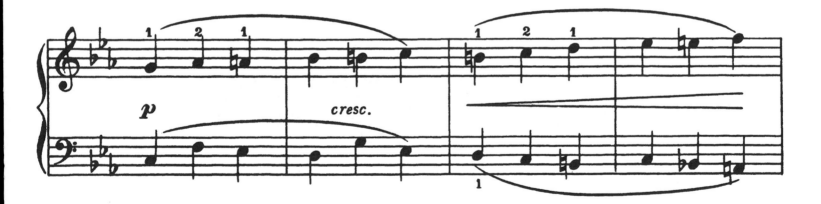

Minuet in D minor

No. 13

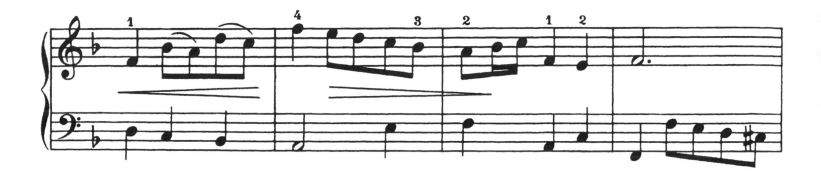

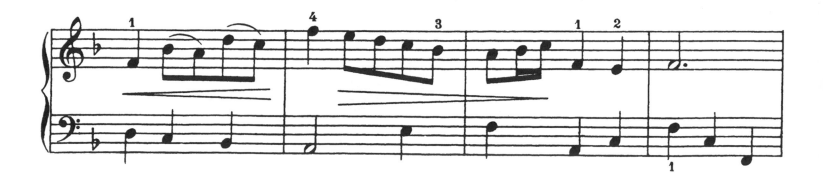

Chorale

Gieb dich zufrieden.

No. 14

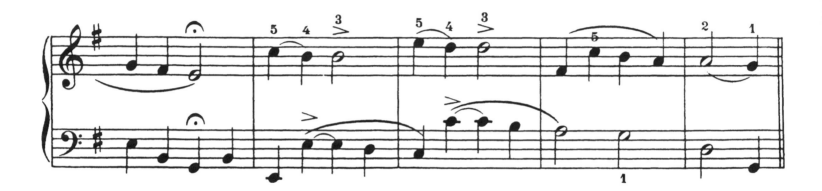

This favorite chorale is said by Spitta to be "one of the most expressive melodies in existence." Other arrangements of it occur in the "Note Book."

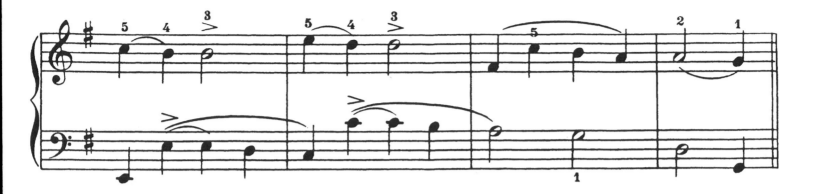

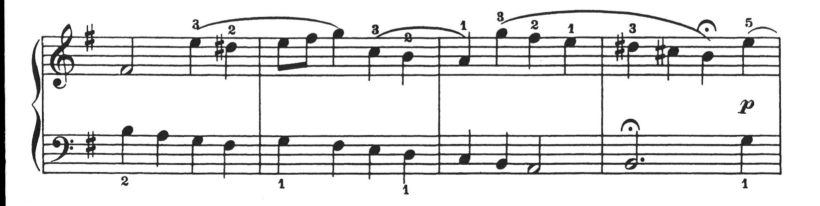

March in G Major

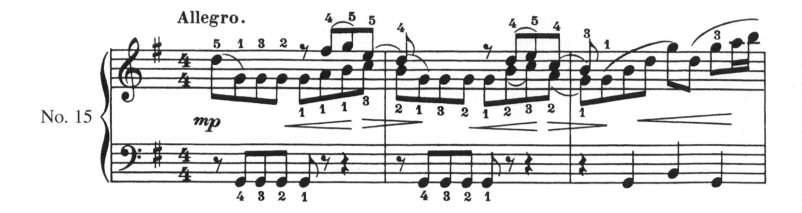

No. 15

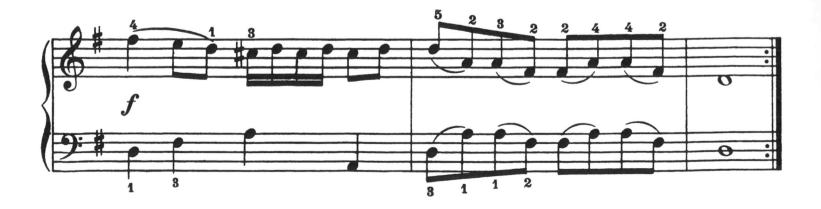

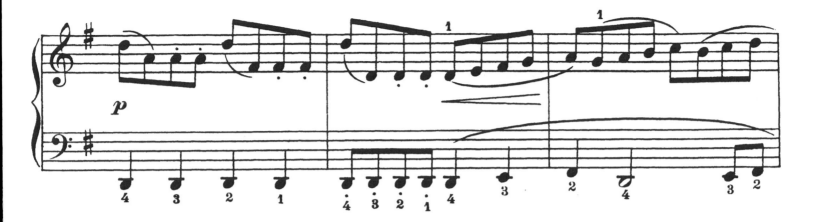

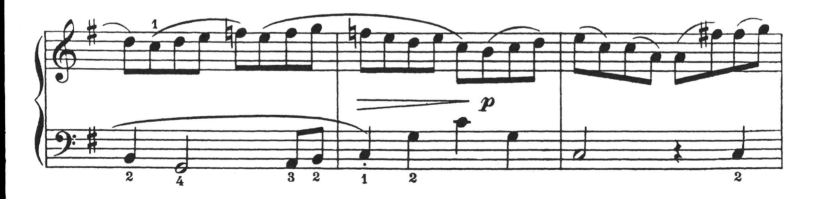

BACH FOR BEGINNERS
Book 2

Preambulum

Compiled and Selected by
CHARLES VINCENT

No. 16

This prelude appears twice in *The Little Clavier Book*, once with embellishments and slightly different to this version.

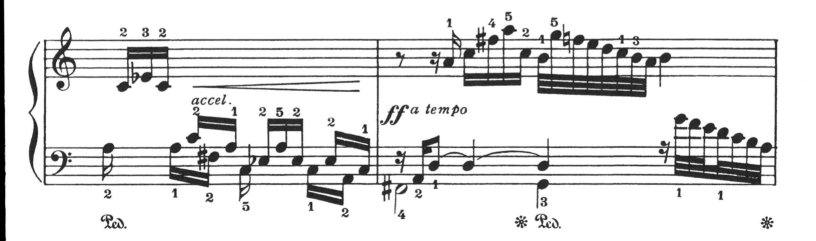

Bourrée

No. 17

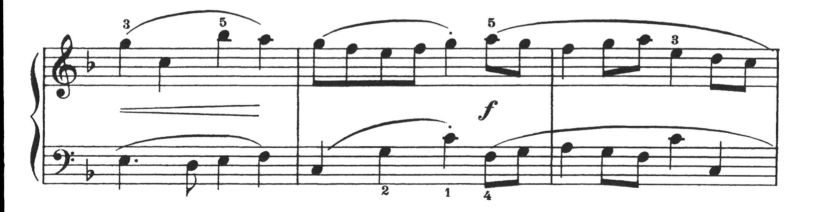

rit. dim.

Gigue

No. 18

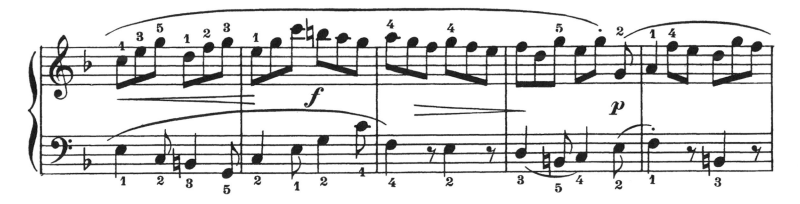

From Overture No. 4.

Prelude in C Major

No. 19

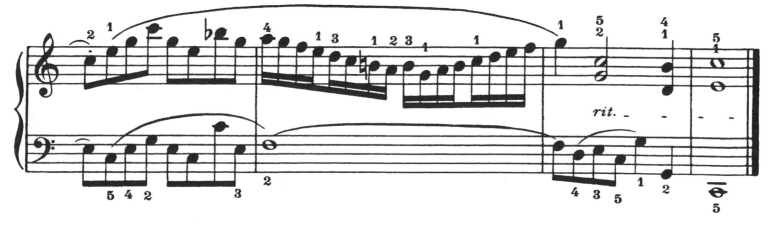

Trio

Andante con espress.

No. 20

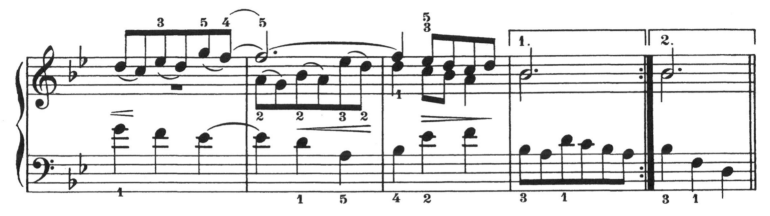

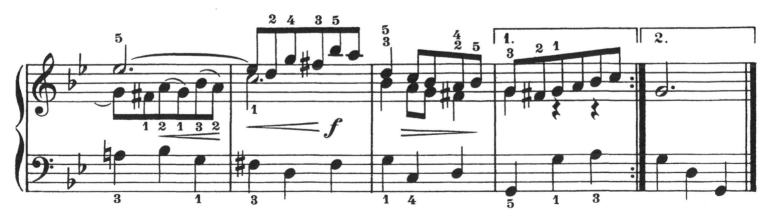

Bach wrote this in *The Little Clavier Book* as a trio to a menuet by Stölzel.

Prelude in D minor

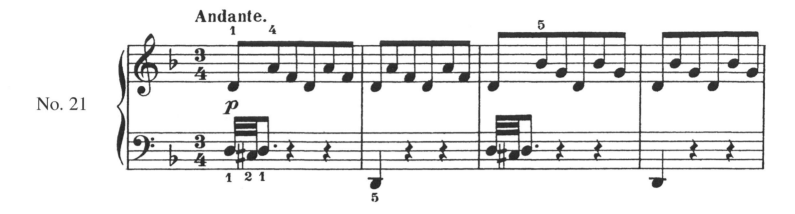

No. 21

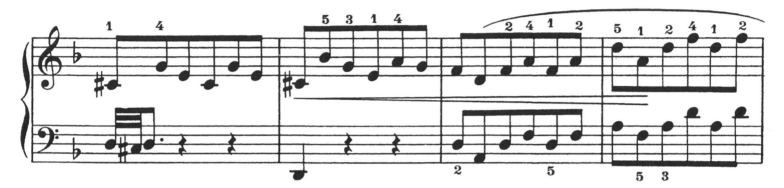

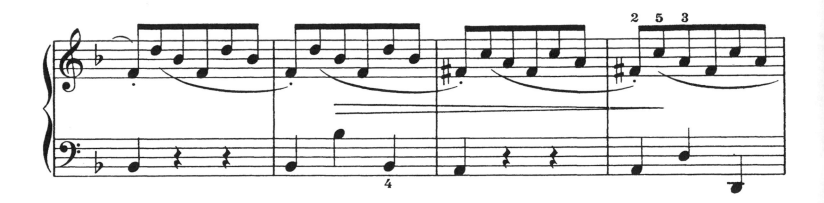

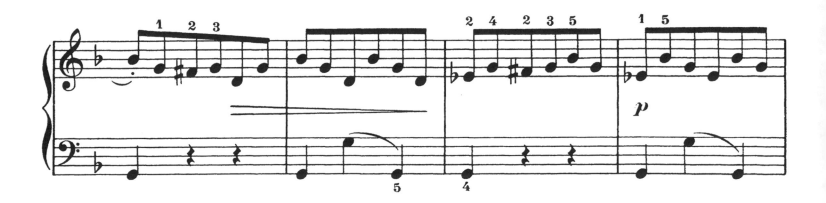

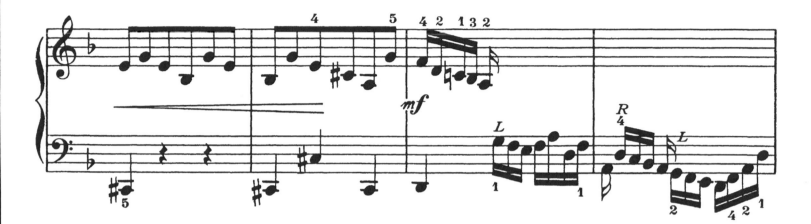

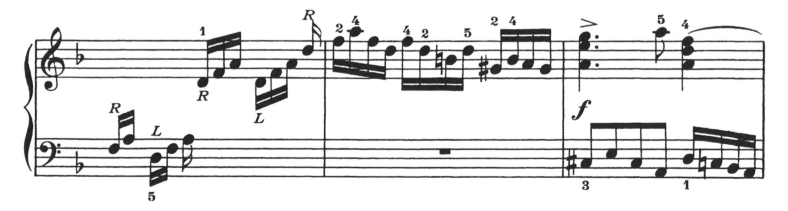

Minuet in G minor

Moderato con espress.

No. 22

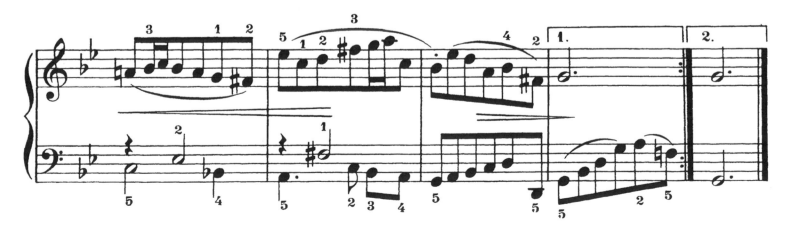

This page is intentionally left blank to facilitate page turns.

Gigue

No. 23

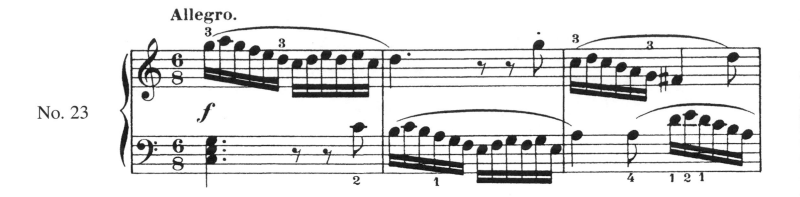

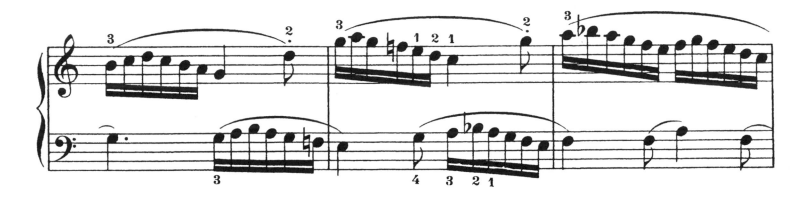

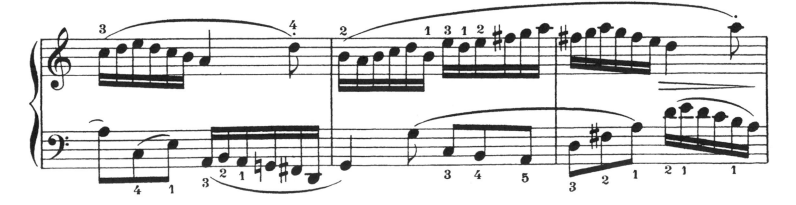

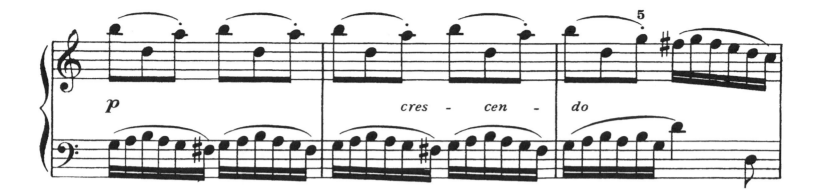

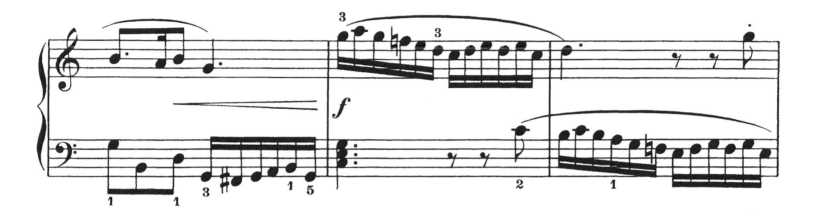

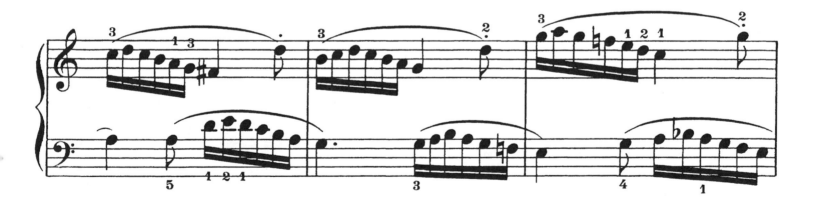

Prelude in F Major

No. 24

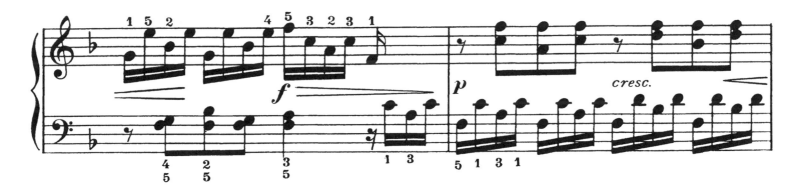

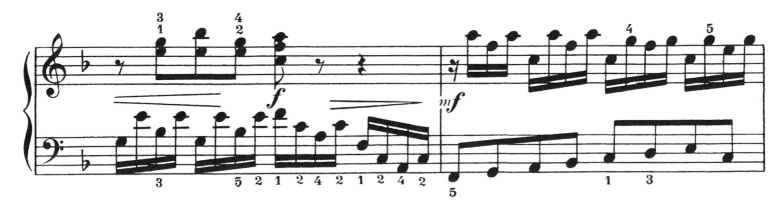

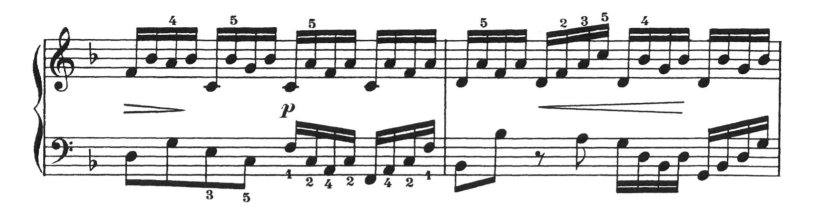

Gigue

Allegro moderato.

No. 25

Originally written in $\frac{3}{8}$ time and in the key of F minor.

Preludium

No. 26

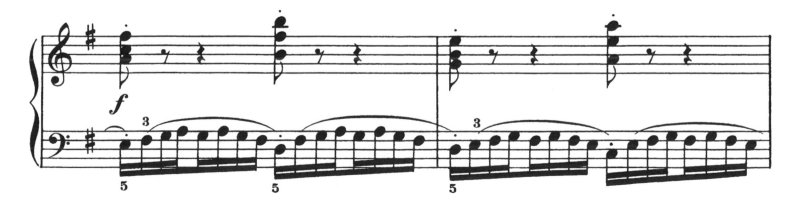

Bach wrote this fine left hand finger study in *The Little Clavier Book* as an exercise for his son, he afterwards developed and elaborated it as No. 10 Prelude in the 18 Preludes and Fugues.

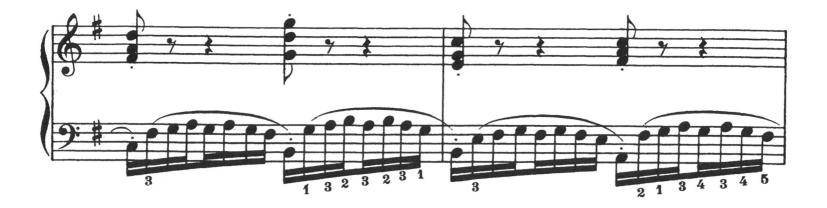

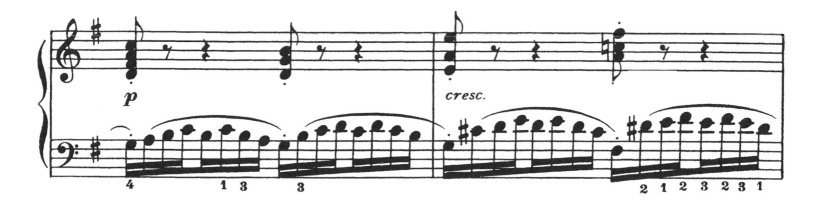

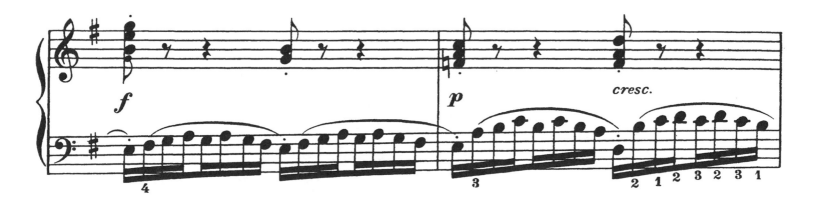

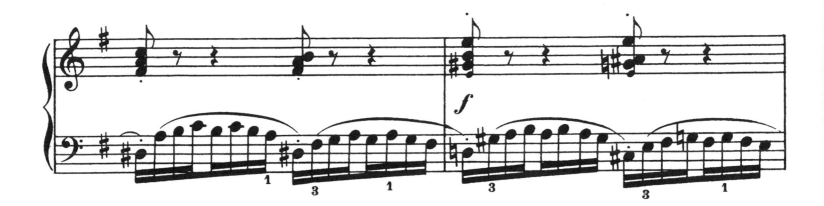

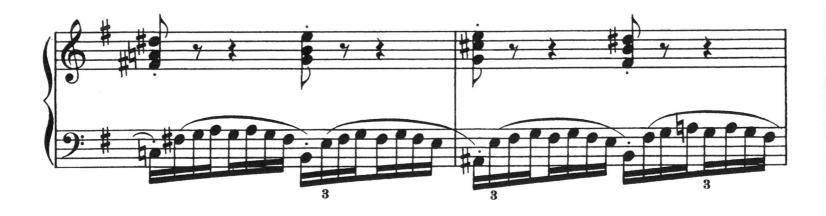

Aria

Moderato.

No. 27

This aria is founded on the notes played by the post horn.
Bach followed it by an interesting fugue on the postillion's theme.

Explanation of the Ornaments or Grace notes.

᷋ **The Upper Mordent** (Pralltrille) is a rapid trill with the diatonic degree next above the chief sound.

written   *played*

᷋ **The Under Mordent** (Mordent) has the trill with (generally) the diatonic degree next below the principal sound.

written   *played*

Chromatic inflections are generally indicated by accidentals placed above or below the Mordent.

written   *played*   or   *played*

᷋ **The Double Mordent** is twice as long as the ordinary Mordent.

written   *played*   *written*   *played*

᷋ A shake or double mordent approached by the note immediately above the principal sound.

written   *played*   or

᷋ A shake or double mordent approached by the note immediately below the principal sound.

written   *played*

The shake generally terminates on the principal sound but when a turn like ending is desired the following signs are employed ᷋ ᷋ ᷋ .

In the Little Clavier Book these examples are given.

written   *played*   *written*   *played*

Much valuable information on the subject of Ornaments can be obtained from "Studies in Musical Graces" by Ernest Fowles.

Applicatio

The fingering in the above study is that written by Bach, and is perhaps more interesting than useful. As this number is introduced more as an application of the various embellishments, it will be left to the discretion of the teacher if the student learns to play it or not.

Prelude in G minor

No. 29

This is an especially interesting prelude, containing as it does
Bach's own fingering and many examples of the upper and
lower mordents.

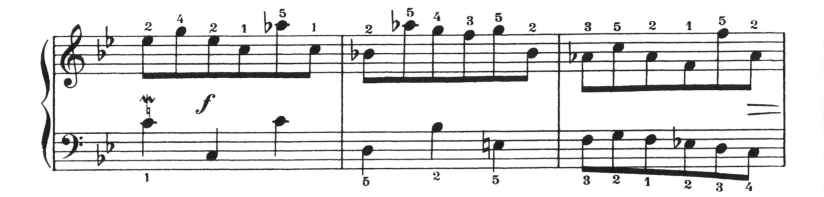

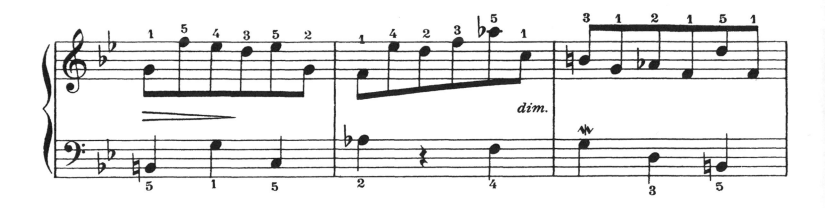

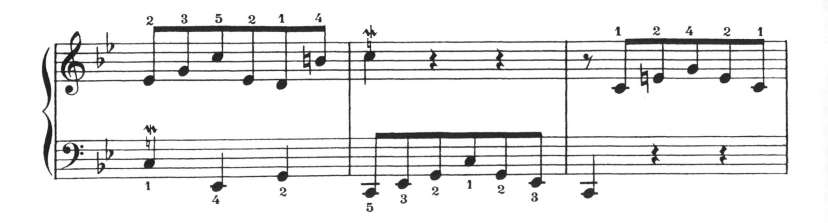

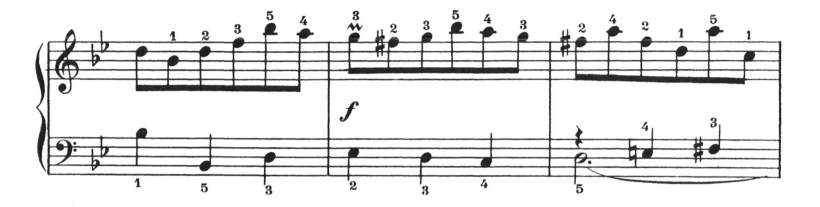

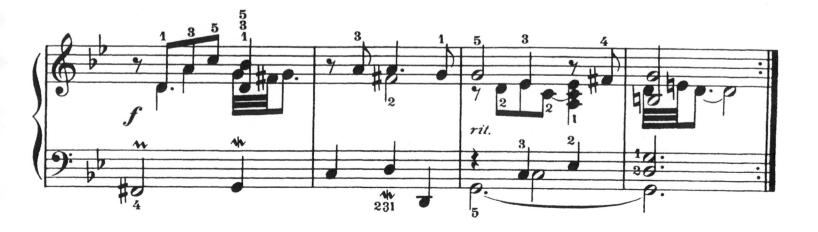